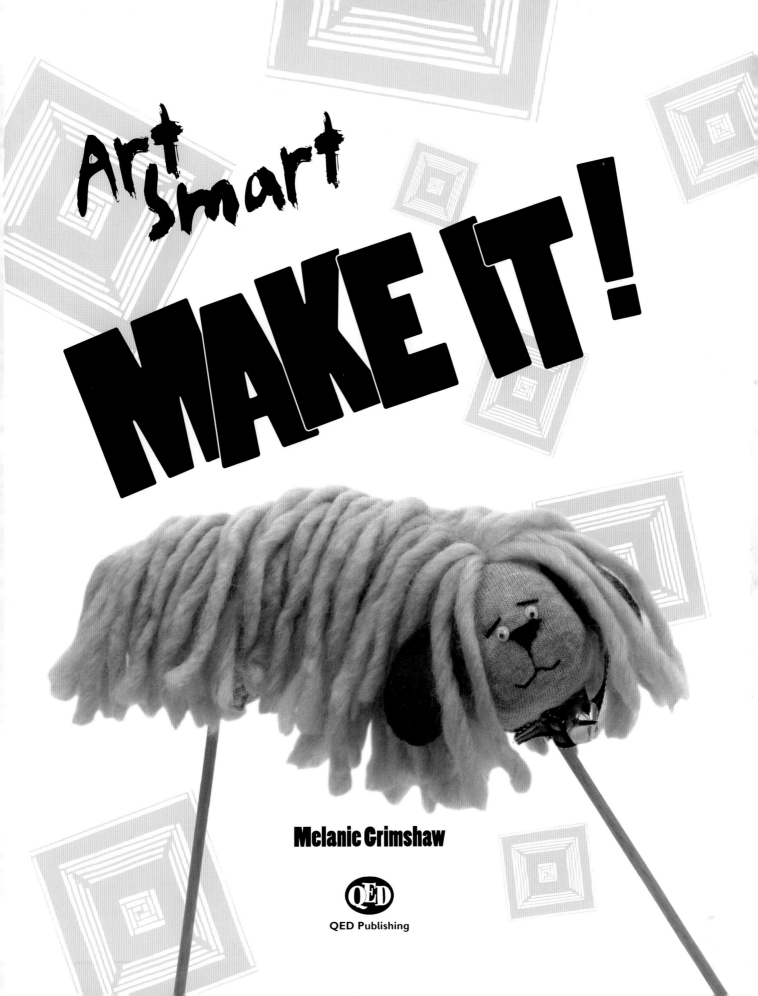

Art smart

MAKE IT!

Melanie Grimshaw

QED

QED Publishing

Editor: Lauren Taylor
Design: Tall Tree Ltd www.talltreebooks.co.uk
Illustrator: Tom Connell
Photography: Philip Wilkins and Mark Winwood

Copyright © QED Publishing 2012

First published in the UK in 2012 by
QED Publishing, a Quarto Group company
230 City Road
London EC1V 2TT

www.qed-publishing.co.uk

A catalogue record for this book is available from the British Library.

ISBN 978 1 84835 865 2

Printed in China

Picture credits
(t=top, b=bottom, l=left, r=right, c=centre, fc=front cover, bc=back cover)
Mark Winwood: 5br, 13b, 25br
Philip Wilkins: 7c, 9b, 11l, 15br, 17bl, 19b, 21bl, 23br, 27b,
Shutterstock: fctl, bctl, akiyoko; fctl SeDmi; fctl oksix; fctc, bctr, oksana2010; fctr Madlen; fcc, bctl, bctc, Iwona Grodzka; fccr, bctr, Kitch Bain; fctr, 3cl, 4c SeDmi; fcc, bcb, 3tr, 20tr, 20br, 14t, 14c, 31bl, Jenny Solomon; fcbl, bccl, 3cr, 22tc, 22br, Garsya; fcbl, 3bl, 24br, Vasily Kovalev; fcbr, 6, 26br, 30tr Picsfive; fccl, bctc, 10cl pukach; 3tl, 3cb, 18cr jcjgphotography; 3br Denis and Yulia Pogostins; 8tr Picsfive; 10cr, 16tr shutswis; 13tl magicoven; 16br, 26tc, pukach

Note to Adults:
Some children might be able to do some or all of these projects on their own, while others might need more help. These are ideas that you can work on together, not only to avoid any problems or accidents, but also to share in the fun of making art.

At the top of the page for each project you will find this handy key. It will tell you the difficulty level to expect from each project:

Quick creative fix
These projects are quick, easy and perfect for a beginner.

Sharpen your skills
Confident with your beginner skills? Move onto these slightly tougher projects.

Ready for a challenge
For a challenging project you can really get stuck into.

Creative masterpiece
Think you can tackle the toughest textile projects? Have a go at these.

CONTENTS

LOVE-HEART GIFT BOX

Is a special occasion coming up? This cute gift box will be a great way to present your gift!

YOU WILL NEED:

- Scissors
- Felt in assorted colours
- Pins
- Needle
- Embroidery thread
- Toy stuffing
- Ribbon
- Cardboard box with lid
- Fabric glue
- Buttons and any decorations you like, such as feathers or sequins.

1 For the heart, cut out two equal-sized pieces of felt. Pin these two pieces together.

2 Using a needle and thread, stitch the heart pieces together using blanket stitch. Leave a small space to insert your toy stuffing, then stitch it completely closed when you have stuffed the heart.

3 Wrap a length of ribbon around the outside of your box, and secure it with fabric glue. You could also stitch on one or two separate felt heart shapes to the ribbon.

4 Gather a length of ribbon together in loops to create a flower shape. Stitch a button in the centre to hold the ribbon in place.

5 Finally, glue the stuffed felt heart and ribbon flower to the box lid using fabric glue.

Make an Easter-themed box using colourful feathers for a cute Easter chick!

WOVEN MOBILE

This mobile will add a splash of colour to your bedroom, and it's great fun to make!

1 With the end of a small ball of wool, tie a knot around the centre of two dowel rods. Secure the rods into a cross shape.

2 Weave the wool over and around one dowel rod, then over and around the next, and so on with each rod. Make sure to keep the wool taut and keep your rods in the cross position.

3 Keep weaving and tie on new colours of wool to make a stripy effect. Stop when you have a few centimetres of space left at both ends of each rod. Tie the loose end of the wool in a knot to secure it.

4 Make a variety of different-sized woven crosses and tie them together with wool to make a hanging mobile. Finally, thread colourful beads onto any loose ends of wool for decoration.

You can use different colours to match the colours of your bedroom!

SPACE PILLOWCASE

Want to create a theme for your bedroom? Printing on fabric can liven up plain pillowcases.

YOU WILL NEED:

- Scissors
- Large piece of cardboard
- A plain pillowcase
- Fabric paints in different colours
- Paper plates
- Various shaped and textured objects for printing
- An iron (and an adult to help you!)
- A thin cloth

1 Cut a piece of cardboard to fit inside your pillowcase. Insert the cardboard into the pillowcase and lie it flat.

2 Squeeze different fabric paint colours onto separate paper plates.

3 Use objects, such as sponges, cotton spools and cardboard shapes, to print with. Dip them into the paint and press them onto the fabric. You can cut out rocket ship or star shapes from sponge and cardboard.

4 Print your pattern all over the front of the pillowcase. Once dry, turn over and repeat on the back.

5 Once completely dry, ask an adult to place a thin cloth over the pillowcase and slowly iron over it on a cool setting. This will seal the paint and stop it from cracking or washing off.

Get creative and use any colours and printing objects you like. How about a nature pattern?

POCKET ORGANIZER

Keep your bedroom tidy and stylish at the same time with this fun organizer.

YOU WILL NEED:

- Scissors
- An old piece of clothing that has pockets
- Felt in assorted colours
- Pins
- Needle
- Embroidery thread
- Fabric glue
- Sequins and goggly eyes
- Long length of ribbon
- Wooden dowel rod

1 Cut a large rectangle from an old piece of clothing, including the pockets.

2 Cut out decorative felt shapes and pin these in place on the fabric. Stick on goggly eyes if you have made any animal shapes.

leaves

animal shapes

eyes

10

3 Stitch on the shapes using running stitch. You can also glue or stitch on sequins to decorate your shapes.

4 Using running stitch, sew a length of ribbon around the edge of the organizer to hide the rough edges and create a border.

5 Stitch two loops of ribbon to the top of the organizer and slip a wooden dowel rod through the loops so it can be hung.

Create felt shapes that show your favourite theme. The more colourful, the better!

HAIR BAND BIRD

You can create this cute, colourful bird for a show-stopping hair accessory.

YOU WILL NEED:

- Scissors
- Felt in assorted colours
- Pins
- Needle
- Embroidery thread
- Toy stuffing
- Fabric glue
- Feathers
- Goggly eyes
- Hair band

1 Cut out two equal-sized pieces of felt for the main body shape of your bird. Pin these two pieces together.

body pieces

2 Using a needle and thread, stitch around the outside of the body in either blanket or running stitch, leaving a space of about **1** centimetre open.

3 Through this space, fill the body with toy stuffing, then stitch up the hole.

4 Cut out felt ovals for the face, a folded diamond for the beak and triangles for the feathers and ears. Glue or stitch these onto the body.

feathers

ears

eyes

beak

face

5 Attach feathers for wings and a pair of goggly eyes to make your bird come to life! Finally, stitch a hair band to the back of the bird's body.

Make a pencil tidy, using different felt shapes and colours to create any animal you want!

GET WELL CARD

This cute, colourful card will really brighten someone's day.

1 Lay three of the felt squares side by side and sew them together in turn, using running stitch. Do this by holding two squares together and stitching along the very edge of one side. Repeat with the third square.

2 Repeat with the other squares to make three rows. Sew the rows together in the same way. Flip the quilt over so the stitching is on the back. Add running stitch around the edge for decoration.

14

3 Make a small pillowcase by cutting out a rectangle of white felt and decorating around the edge in running stitch.

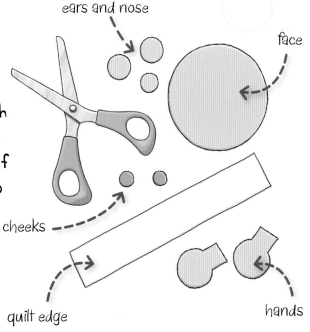

ears and nose

face

cheeks

quilt edge

hands

4 Cut out felt shapes for the face and hands. Stitch eyes and a mouth onto the face circle and glue this onto the pillowcase. Cut a strip of white felt to make a quilt edge to position the hands onto.

5 Using an embroidery needle, sew wool around the head to make hair. Glue all the felt pieces onto a rectangle of backing felt and glue onto a folded piece of A4 card.

Who wouldn't feel better after receiving a beautiful card like this?

DINO DOORSTOP

This colourful fabric dinosaur will make the perfect little guard for your bedroom door.

1 With tailors' chalk, draw four equal-sided triangles on the patterned fabrics and felt. Make sure each side of each triangle is 15 cm long. Cut out the triangles.

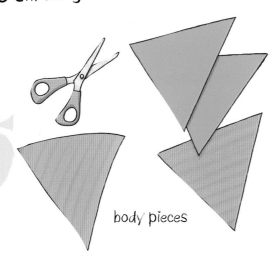

body pieces

2 With the patterned sides facing inward, use running stitch to sew the triangles together at the sides to make a pyramid shape. Leave the final side open and turn the pyramid the right way around.

3 Through the open side, fill the pyramid with dried beans. (You can use a paper cone to do this.) Sew up the open side with blanket stitch.

tail

claws

4 Make a stuffed felt snout, two hands and a tail using felt shapes sewn together with running stitch and stuffed with toy stuffing. Stitch these pieces onto the pyramid body.

5 Cut out features, such as spikes, teeth, claws, eyebrows and spots, from felt and a sheet of foam. Glue these onto the body, then stick on a pair of goggly eyes to bring your dinosaur to life!

Make a cuddly dinosaur instead by replacing the dried beans with toy stuffing.

TWISTY SOCK SNAKE

This twisty snake is cute, colourful and super-easy to make.

1 Fill a sock with toy stuffing and insert a pipe cleaner through the middle, so it is contained inside.

2 Tie about six elastic bands at 5 centimetre intervals along the sock to create the round sections of the snake's body.

3 Sew a line of loose running stitch around the opening and pull the end of the thread until it gathers closed. Secure by tying a knot in the thread.

4 Cut out felt shapes to add to your snake, such as a pink forked tongue and diamond shapes to decorate its back. Sew or glue these into position.

eyes

diamond shapes

tongue

5 Finally, add some finishing touches to your snake. Sew on colourful beads for decoration and add goggly eyes to bring him to life.

A patterned sock will make your snake even more interesting.

PATCHWORK PICTURE

Pictures don't have to be painted. You can create a 3D picture using fabrics instead.

YOU WILL NEED:

- An A5 wooden picture frame, glass and backing removed
- String
- Staple gun and staples
- Scissors
- Paper
- Pins
- Assorted green, patterned fabrics
- Green and black felt
- Needle
- Embroidery thread
- Toy stuffing
- Long length of blue and purple wool and ribbon
- Fabric glue
- 2 x White and grey pom poms (see page 28)

1 Wrap string around your frame, leaving 1-centimetre spaces between the lengths. Staple the threads to the back of the frame and cut off the lengths at the front.

2 Cut out about five hill shapes from paper and use these as templates to cut out hills from patterned fabrics and felt. Make sure the hills will fit in the lower half of your frame.

20

3 Sew the fabric hills onto a 20 x 8-centimetre rectangle of green felt, using running stitch. Leave a space in each to insert a small amount of toy stuffing before sewing them closed. Trim the top of the backing felt into a curved hill shape.

4 To make the sky, weave the ribbon and wool through the lengths of string on the frame until half the frame is filled.

head

pom pom body

5 For the sheep, glue two pom poms to the hills. Cut out black felt heads and glue them into position. Finally, staple your hill landscape, facedown, to the back of your frame.

Why not try making a picture of the scene outside your window?

HESSIAN POT WRAP

Work on your embroidery skills and brighten up a dull flower pot with this pretty wrap.

YOU WILL NEED:

- 40 x 40 cm square of hessian fabric
- Flower pot
- Ribbon
- Tailors' chalk
- Needle
- Embroidery thread in assorted colours
- Assorted beads and buttons

1 Gather the hessian fabric around the flower pot and tie it up at the top with a ribbon tied into a bow.

2 Using the tailors' chalk, draw a tree design on one side of the hessian fabric. At the ends of the tree branches, draw circular shapes.

3 Begin your embroidery by using back stitch to outline the tree trunk. Embroider the circles using colourful thread and a variety of stitches, such as chain stitch and satin stitch.

4 Sew on assorted beads and buttons to add a decorative finish.

Wrapped around a beautiful plant, this would make a wonderful Mother's Day gift.

BOUNCY BIRD

Hang this feathered friend next to your window in your room.

YOU WILL NEED:

- 2 small elastic bands
- Polystyrene ball
- Wool in assorted colours
- Embroidery needle
- Scissors
- Beads in assorted colours
- Felt in assorted colours
- Needle
- Embroidery thread
- Toy stuffing
- Fabric Glue
- Feathers
- Goggly eyes
- Length of elastic thread

1 Wrap two elastic bands around a polystyrene ball so they cross over each other. Using wool threaded onto an embroidery needle, thread the wool over and around the elastic bands. (See page 6 for a similar method.)

2 Keep weaving until the ball is covered, changing wool colours to make a stripy effect. Tie a knot in your last thread and cut off the excess. You could leave some wool threads loose to attach beads for decoration.

3 Make a pair of wings by cutting out four identical wing shapes from felt. Sew the pairs together with running stitch. Leave a space to insert a small amount of toy stuffing, then sew closed.

4 To make a tail, glue feathers onto the back of your bird. Glue the stiff quills under a section of woven wool. Glue or sew the wings onto the sides of the body.

5 Glue on on a folded diamond felt beak and add goggly eyes. Stitch a length of elastic thread to the ridge at the top so you can hang your bird.

Make your bird in colours that match your bedroom!

POOCH PUPPET

This soft puppet is just as cute and cuddly as a real dog – but not as much work!

YOU WILL NEED:

- A sock
- Toy stuffing
- Pipe cleaner
- 3 elastic bands
- Needle
- Embroidery thread in assorted colours
- Large embroidery needle
- About 40 x 10 cm-lengths of thick wool
- Scissors
- Brown felt
- Goggly eyes
- Fabric glue
- Small bell
- Ribbon
- 2 wooden dowel rods

1 Fill a sock with toy stuffing and insert a pipe cleaner through the middle, so it is contained inside. Tie 3 elastic bands at regular spaces to create round body sections.

2 Sew a line of loose running stitch around the opening and pull the end of the thread until the opening gathers together.

3 Sew a line of running stitch all the way down the back of the sock body.

4 To make the pooch's fur, thread each length of wool through the running stitches along the back, using a large embroidery needle. Embroider a nose, mouth and eyebrows onto the face. Stick on goggly eyes.

5 Cut out two felt ears and sew these onto the head. Sew the bell onto a length of ribbon and tie around the pooch's neck. Finally, make a small hole in the underside of the head, and push one dowel rod into the hole. Repeat at the other end of the body.

Make a family of pooches using different coloured socks and wool.

MATERIALS

wool

embroidery thread

Embroidery thread

This is a type of yarn used especially for embroidery. It comes in loads of different colours.

Needles and pins

pins

Needles are pointed metal tools to sew with. They have a hole at the top called an 'eye' to thread yarn through. Pins are very similar to needles but don't have an eye at the top. They are used to hold fabric in place before sewing. Always ask an adult to help you with needles and pins. They can be very sharp.

needle

fabric paint

Wool

Wool is like very thick yarn that comes in many different colours and thicknesses. It is usually used for knitting, but can be used for weaving and even embroidery.

Toy stuffing

This is soft, white material, similar to cotton wool. It is great for padding out your creations, to help them look more 3D. It also makes toys soft and cuddly!

toy stuffing

Fabric paint

Fabric paints are best for painting onto fabric, as they will not wash off or bleed into the material. They will need fixing with a hot iron before washing, but always make sure an adult does this for you. Make sure whatever you are painting onto has been washed first.

Dowel rods

Dowel rods are solid, lightweight sticks used for adding support to your creations. They are usually made of wood or plastic. They are easy to cut to size, but always ask an adult to do this for you.

dowel rods

Tailors' chalk

Tailors' chalk is a very hard type of chalk that is used to make marks on fabric. It is useful to draw out shapes that you need to cut out. The marks can be washed off.

tailors' chalk

Felt

This is a type of cloth that is usually soft and comes in loads of different colours. It is strong and will not fray when cut.

Foam sheets

These are thick sheets of a lightweight but tough, bendy material. You can cut them into shapes, glue them and bend them without them tearing.

foam sheet

Fabric

fabrics

Fabric is any type of cloth. You can use old clothes to make your creations from, but always ask an adult before cutting anything up!

Glue

The types of glue you'll need most when doing creative projects are PVA glue and fabric glue. PVA glue is good for sticking down paper, card, wood and almost anything. Fabric glue is better to stick fabrics, as can be washed without coming unstuck.

felt

glue

TECHNIQUES

MAKE A POM POM

YOU WILL NEED:
- Scissors
- Cardboard
- Wool

1 Cut two identical doughnut rings from cardboard and place them together.

2 Wrap the wool around the rings, going through the hole and around the outer edge. Keep wrapping until the hole in the middle is very tight.

3 Cut through the wool around the edge of the ring, a layer at a time, until you meet the cardboard rings underneath.

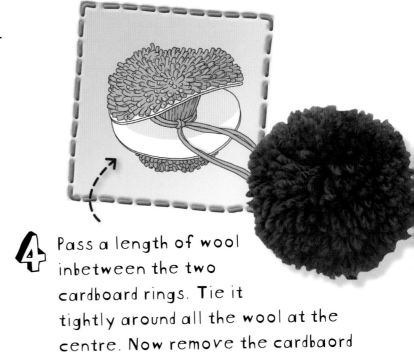

4 Pass a length of wool inbetween the two cardboard rings. Tie it tightly around all the wool at the centre. Now remove the cardbaord rings and reveal your pom pom!

STITCHING AND WEAVING

Running stitch
Sew up and down through the fabric, making sure the stitches on both the topside and underside are kept the same size.

Blanket stitch
Push the needle through from back to front. At the front, level with your first stitch, push the needle through the fabric but come up again by going through the loop you have created with the thread.

Back stitch
Make a running stitch, then come up through the fabric a stitch ahead and stitch backwards to meet your first running stitch. Repeat in a neat line.

Weaving
Lengths of material are passed through a set of taut, spaced-out threads, in an alternate 'over, under, over, under' pattern. This is repeated with many lengths so that they make an interlacing lattice. You can also weave 'over and around' dowel rods in a cross shape (see woven mobile on page 6).

Chain stitch
Come up through the fabric and make a little loop, held in place with your thumb. Go back down through the fabric at the top and inside the loop. Come back up and forward a stitch length. Before pulling the needle all the way out, wrap the free thread under the needle and pull out to create your second loop.

Satin stitch
Mark out the shape you want and sew straight stitches closely together across the shape, taking care to keep the edges even.

INDEX